An Executive Summary of

Peter Schiff's

The Real Crash: America's Coming Bankruptcy—How to Save Yourself and Your Country

By A. D. Thibeault

D1416807

Table of Contents

i. Introduction/Synopsis

PART I: THE PROBLEM

1. Big Government Is the Problem, Not the Solution

- The Financial Crash of 2008

2. The Federal Reserve, and the Manipulation of the Interest Rate

3. The Bubble, and the Pop (and the Re–Bubble)

4. The Coming Crash

- a. Government Debt

- b. The Danger of Growing Debt

5. How America Could Have Avoided the Coming Crash

6. Why It's Too Late to Avoid the Crash Now

- a. Government Stimulus Can't Save the Country

- b. The Government Should Declare Bankruptcy

PART II: THE SOLUTION

Section 1: Curtailing Social Services & Government Regulations

7. Health Care

8. Social Security

9. Education

- a. K–12

- b. Higher Education

10. The Military

11. Private Sector Regulations

- a. The Financial Industry

- b. Broad Regulations: Minimum Wage and Anti–
  Discrimination Laws

Section 2: The Gold Standard, Tax Reform, and Localizing
Government

12. Reinstituting the Gold Standard

- a. A Short History of the Federal Reserve

13. Tax Reform

14. Localizing Government

15. Conclusion

i. Introduction/Synopsis

Since the housing and financial crash of 2008, America's recovery has been tepid at best. Unemployment has remained high;

manufacturing has not returned; personal savings are as low as they've ever been, and personal debt as high; housing is still a mess, and banking not much better; and, to top it all off, government debt is awe–inspiring and seems completely insoluble. According to financial investor, commentator and author Peter Schiff, while all of this is certainly disheartening, it should not come as much of a surprise. Indeed, Schiff argues that all of this economic slumping is a natural result of America's misguided economic policies; including especially the Federal Reserve's manipulation of interest rates, the government's uncontrollable borrowing, and, in connection with this, the maintaining (and even expansion) of unsustainable social programs . For Schiff, these same policies led directly to the crash of '08 (which he correctly and very famously predicted), and are leading the U.S. directly into an even worse crash now. In his new book *The Real Crash: America's Coming Bankruptcy—how to Save Yourself and Your Country* Schiff outlines how America got itself into this mess in the first place, what the end game is likely to be, and what the nation and its citizens should do to make the coming unpleasantness the least unpleasant as possible.

The main problem—and where most of the other problems begin—according to Schiff, is the Fed's manipulation of interest rates. By interfering with the free market value of money, and making it cheaper than the market would dictate, the Fed encourages financial bubbles that then necessarily pop. When a bubble pops, the market needs to correct itself; however, over the past 20 years, the Fed has not really allowed this correction to take place, as every time a bubble pops the Fed has lowered the interest rate even further, causing more money to enter the system and a new bubble to form. First it was dot–com stocks, then it was housing, and now it is government spending.

As a matter of fact, while government spending has reached new and mind–boggling heights in the recent past, it has actually been ballooning in this direction for years, spurred on largely by the low–interest rates that the Fed has provided. The government has used this borrowed money to establish social programs (such as Social Security and Medicare), and, more recently, bailout packages for failing businesses and entire industries. All the while, the government has been going deeper and deeper into debt. A big part of what has allowed the American government to borrow as much as it has (and to keep on borrowing now) is the fact that the American dollar is the world's reserve currency, which means it is always in demand, and hence people and organizations have been willing to act as creditors in order to get it. For Schiff, though, the sheer size of the debt, and the fact that it is running away faster and faster everyday (and has no realistic chance of ever being repaid) will sooner or later turn investors away from considering the American dollar a valuable reserve—at which point it will lose its status as the world's reserve, and investors will stop investing in it.

At this point, the American government will have but two options. It can either declare bankruptcy, or it can print the money it needs to pay its debt. In either case, an enormous crash will result, for in the first case, an astronomical sum of money that the economy had assumed existed will suddenly be wiped away, and in the latter case hyperinflation will set in, and the American dollar will be whittled down to worthless.

At this point, the country will be forced to start over. For Schiff, this may not be such a bad thing, for, according to him, the nation has simply put itself in an unsustainable position, and the sooner it starts over the better. At that time, Schiff argues, America can finally get back to the small government and free–market forces that the country's founding fathers designed the nation around. While much of the book is focused on how the country can do this now, before the crash hits (in such areas as banking & finance, taxation, healthcare, education, the military, et. al.), Schiff very much believes that nothing can actually prevent the crash from coming, and that therefore, most of the rebuilding will have to be done after The Real Crash.

Here is Peter Schiff speaking about his new book:
http://www.youtube.com/watch?v=-s7EKsWV7IY&feature=related

What follows is a full executive summary of *The Real Crash: America's Coming Bankruptcy—how to Save Yourself and Your Country* by Peter Schiff. (Just a word of warning: in the book, Schiff does occasionally give the reader general investment advice based on his analysis and prognostications. However, this is very much a secondary concern of his, and therefore, I have not included it here. If you wish to learn more about Schiff's investment advice you may wish to peruse his website here: http://www.europac.net/ or consult his investment firm directly).

PART I: THE PROBLEM

1. Big Government Is the Problem, Not the Solution

In essence, the solutions that Schiff prescribes to help solve America's economic problems involve shrinking government as much as possible. For Schiff, this boils down to two principles: "1. Government shouldn't do anything that individuals or the private sector can do; 2. If government involvement is needed, the involvement should be as local as possible" (loc. 4743). Now, Schiff is fully aware that this is precisely the opposite approach that is advocated by most elements of the mainstream media and political community. Indeed, the author repeatedly points out that every time something goes wrong with the economy, journalists and politicians alike tend to blame the free market, and propose more government as the solution (loc. 1533). For Schiff, though, what the pundits consistently fail to appreciate is that the American system contains a mix of free–market principles and government interference, and, more often than not, it is the latter that is causing the country's problems.

a. The Financial Crash of 2008

Take the financial crash of 2008, for instance. As Schiff reminds us, "journalists and politicians agreed that 'unfettered free markets' caused the crash and the ensuing suffering. This became an excuse for more laws and regulations, meaning more power for politicians, bureaucrats, and central bankers. Regulation, we were told, would make the economy safe" (loc. 595). In this particular instance, many experts agreed that a major contributing factor to the crash was the Gramm–Leach–Biley Act of 1999, which had repealed a government regulation (known as Glass–Steagall) that had prevented commercial banks from acting as investment banks (loc. 1694). In other words, people blamed the freeing up of the market for the problem. For Schiff, though, this explanation fails to take into account the whole story.

To begin with, Schiff points out that the Glass–Steagall regulation mentioned above was only a part of the government bill known as the Glass–Steagall Act (named after the two senators, Carter Glass and Henry Steagall, who proposed it) that was enacted in 1933 (loc. 1694). In fact, the regulation in question was only a secondary aspect of the bill. The main proviso of the bill stipulated that the government would insure the holdings of depositors in commercial banks up to a certain point—under the aegis of the Federal Deposit Insurance Corporation (FDIC) (loc. 1569, 1594). The FDIC was meant to re–instill confidence in banks, which confidence had been rocked after the bank runs at the beginning of the Great Depression in the previous years (loc. 1569). As Schiff explains, the lawmakers knew that the government's insuring deposits would open up the possibility that the banks would become overly risky with these deposits (since if they knew that they would be bailed out, there would be less incentive to avoid risk) (loc. 1702). In order to protect against this, the legislators included the restriction against how banks could operate. When Glass–Steagall was repealed by the Clinton administration in 1999, the restriction against banks was removed, but the government's insurance of deposits was preserved (loc. 1702). In other words, the moral hazard caused by one aspect of the bill was preserved, while the check on this moral hazard was removed. For Schiff, then, it was not the removal of a government restriction that caused the problem, but the fact that another government regulation was left to skew the system unchecked.

Of course, this just pushes the argument back to the government regulation on insuring depositors' holdings. While many would argue that this regulation is ultimately beneficial, Schiff denies that this is the case. According to him, the behaviour of banks would in fact be kept in check much better by the forces at work in a truly free market (loc. 1715–40). For one thing, Schiff argues, banking insurance would not vanish, but would simply be taken over by the private sector, which, according to the author, would be able to handle it much more efficiently: "without the FDIC, bank deposit insurance would not disappear, but risk would still bear a cost. Private deposit insurers would arise, and risk become more accurately priced" (loc. 1714).

2. The Federal Reserve, and the Manipulation of the Interest Rate

Now, for Schiff, while the FDIC certainly played a large part in the financial crash of 2008, there is another way that the government interferes in the economy which played an even larger part, and that is the Federal Reserve's manipulation of the interest rate. Indeed, while Schiff maintains that less government regulation is generally the right approach for most of our economic problems, he does hold that there are certain areas where government interference is more harmful than others, and top of the list here is the Federal Reserve's manipulation of the interest rate.

As Schiff explains, the interest rate represents the price of borrowing money (loc. 5508). In a free market, prices are determined by supply and demand alone, so in this situation the interest rate is determined by the supply of money available for lending, which, in turn, is determined by the amount of money that has been put into banks in the form of savings (loc. 5510). In the American system, though (as with most modern governments), the interest rate is set by the Central Bank, known in the U.S. as the Federal Reserve. The Fed sets the interest rate by way of dictating the rate at which major banks borrow from it (called the discount rate) (loc. 5514), as well as by influencing the rate at which banks borrow from each other (called the federal–funds rate) (loc 5514). With regards to the latter action, the Fed influences the federal–funds rate by way of impacting how much money is in the system, which it does by way of buying and selling government treasuries and other securities: "by buying up securities, the fed injects more cash into the banking system" (loc. 5514).

Now, the interest rate influences how much people either save, or borrow and spend. For instance, as interest rates go up, people are more likely to save their money, because they can make more of a profit in doing so. By contrast, when interest rates go down, people are more likely to borrow and spend, because they can do so for cheaper, and saving their money does not net them as much of a profit. The degree to which people either save, or borrow and spend influences the growth rate of the economy, for spending tends to spur growth, while saving tends to restrict it (at least in the short term, Schiff would be quick to add). With this knowledge in mind, the Fed manipulates the interest rate in order to regulate the growth rate of the economy (loc. 630–36). For example, if the economy is slowing, or in a downturn, the Fed may wish to lower the interest rate in order to spur borrowing and spending in the hopes that this will jumpstart the economy (loc. 5514). However, Schiff challenges the wisdom of this move.

You see, when the Fed sets the interest rate lower than the market would dictate, people borrow more than they otherwise would, and they then use it to buy more consumer goods, and also go looking to invest it in areas that they think will make money. According to Schiff, though, If the economy is in a downturn when this occurs, then businesses don't look as appealing as they otherwise would (for they are not as profitable during these times) (loc. 188, 5530), and so, the author continues, people tend to put their money into more speculative investments, such as stocks, or any industry that is receiving special treatment from the government (through subsidies or favorable tax discounts) (loc. 5530). But when a glut of money that the free market says should not be around, goes chasing speculative investments, then the money invested tends to balloon them beyond their true value. In other words, you get a bubble.

3. The Bubble, and the Pop (and the Re–Bubble)

Now, easy money is not the only thing that is capable of producing a bubble. Nor is government interference the only factor that has been known to contribute to their formation. Nevertheless, it is one factor that does so (and, Schiff would say, the most important factor nowadays). The more important point is that once a bubble forms, sooner or later, it must pop. That is, eventually people realize that the investment in question has ballooned in value to beyond what it is truly worth, investors rush to pull their money out, and the value of the investment drops. People who were caught holding the investment at the height of the bubble end up selling it for less than they bought it for, and thereby lose money. In the bigger picture, this causes the economy to contract. And the bigger the bubble, the bigger the ensuing contraction.

Now, economic contractions hurt: people spend less, which hurts sales and forces businesses to lay off workers, which causes people to spend even less etc. And the bigger the contraction, the bigger the hurt. For Schiff, though, the contraction at the conclusion of a bubble is a necessary evil. It allows the market to correct itself from a period of excess (loc. 185, 800). Here's how: In a free market the decrease in available money during a contraction causes interest rates to rise (since there is less money around, those who are willing and able to borrow must put up more to get it). The rise in interest rates simultaneously encourages those with money to lend it out to those willing to pay for it (via the banks) in order to earn the higher interest rate (loc. 5549). Also, as money becomes more expensive, its purchasing power increases, so prices drop (loc. 427, 5539). In addition, because unemployment increases, wages drop (loc. 427). Low prices and wages encourage entrepreneurs to invest in their businesses, and eventually you have a recovery.

Now, as Schiff points out, in the past 20 years, every time a bubble has formed and popped, rather than allowing the market to contract, and correct itself, the Fed has instead lowered interest rates, and pumped more money into the economy. So, in the 1990's the Fed poured cheap money into the system resulting in the dot–com stock bubble of 2000 to 2001 (loc. 185). At this point, rather than allowing the economy to contract and correct itself, the Fed lowered interest rates (loc. 190). This, in conjunction with the government's subsidizing the housing market (loc. 866–86, 941–72), caused the cheap cash to flood into housing, thereby preventing a contraction, but also causing another bubble (loc. 187). This was the housing bubble that popped in 2008 (Schiff famously predicted that this bubble would pop years before it actually did [see video below]). When the housing bubble popped, the Fed kept interest rates low once again, and the government swooped in (loc. 193) and used the cheap money to bailout failing businesses, and also expand social programs (including Medicare). For Schiff, government spending is the latest bubble. The problem is that when the government bubble pops there will be nothing left to inflate, and that's when we'll get the real crash (loc. 201).

Here is Peter Schiff predicting the real estate crash of 2008 in 2006 (this is part 1 of 8—the remaining parts are available on YouTube): http://www.youtube.com/watch?v=6G3Qefbt0n4

4. The Coming Crash

So, what makes Schiff so sure that government spending is indeed a bubble, and that it will inevitably crash? Here's why: government debt depends on investors buying government–issued Treasury bills and bonds (or 'Treasuries'), which are essentially promissory notes entitling the owner to a payout when the bill or bond comes due (loc. 209). In the meantime, the government uses the loan to pay for whatever expenses it has.

a. Government Debt

Because the American economy was so strong for so long, and produced so many goods valued by the rest of the world, the American dollar—which one needed in order to buy these goods—became particularly valuable. So valuable in fact, that it became the world's preferred currency, thus earning it the status of the 'reserve currency' of the world (loc. 453). Because the American dollar is so valuable in its role as the world's reserve, many are willing to lend to the American government in order to get it, and the government has been allowed to run up a sizeable debt as a result (loc. 460). Indeed, when we look at the numbers, America's debt currently runs at $17 trillion, which "works out to $140,000 per taxpayer" (loc. 207). In 2010, the interest payments on this debt alone stood at $414 billion (loc. 213). And as the debt grows, the interest payments only get larger.

So, where does the government get the money to pay off its debt, and the interest on this debt? For now, the government is not actually paying off its debt, or the interest on it: it simply borrows more money in order to meet its payments (loc. 209, 453). But this just gets the government further and deeper in debt, so the question recurs: how will the government ever repay its debt? Ultimately, there are only two ways the government can do this: 1) through a combination of decreasing spending and increasing taxes; and 2) by printing off more money.

With regards to the first option, as Schiff points out, the decrease in spending and increase in taxes that the country would need to pay off the debt is truly staggering. For instance, "to simply keep the debt from increasing in 2020, we would need to eliminate all discretionary spending and cut entitlements by 15 percent... Alternatively, we could increase taxes—on everyone, not just rich people—by nearly 50 percent" (loc. 5563). As Schiff explains, the chances of politicians imposing the necessary measures to achieve this before an actual disaster strikes are virtually nil: "we're not likely to do any of these things or any sufficient combination of them, and so the national debt will keep rising, digging us into a deeper hole. Politicians all talk about shrinking the national debt, but there's no reason to believe anyone can actually shrink it—or even slow its growth" (loc. 5570).

As for the second option, the problem with printing more money is that you get inflation; or, considering how much money it would take to pay the present debt, hyperinflation, which is very bad. Indeed, it does nothing less than destroy the value of your currency (loc. 5651), and your economy along with it (loc. 557, 5658). To put it simply then, the government has a debt it cannot pay (loc. 5570).

b. The Danger of Growing Debt

So, if the American government can't pay off its debt, why do creditors keep lending to it? For Schiff, a big part of the reason has to do with the fact that the American dollar is, for the time being, the world's reserve currency (loc. 456). However, as the debt continues to mount, even the dollar's status as the world's reserve will not be able to keep investors from turning away from it. This proves to be the case, according to Schiff, because the government's ability to convince creditors to continue investing in the dollar depends on it both keeping interest rates low and containing inflation (loc. 5623). Interest rates must be kept low, for otherwise the interest payments themselves would become unmanageable, and the government would not be able to pay them (loc. 5628). Inflation must be kept low, for otherwise the value of the dollar is weakened, meaning investors would be paid back in dollars that are worth less and less, thus ultimately making any further investment pointless. Now, while the Fed currently has a policy of keeping interest low and inflation down, Schiff maintains that it does not actually have the power to do so indefinitely (loc. 5621–39). This is because keeping interest rates down below what market forces dictate requires continually pumping money into the system, and doing this inevitably weakens the value of the dollar, meaning you get inflation (loc. 5626–38).

The Consumer Price Index (CPI) currently lists the inflation rate at 3.86 percent (loc. 5510). However, according to Schiff, the way that the CPI is currently calculated underestimates the true value of rising prices: "thanks to the Boskin Commission, the CPI no longer accurately measures price increases. Instead a complex methodology using geometric weighing, substitution, and hedonics results in a CPI that rises more slowly than the general price level (loc. 2578). By Schiff's estimates, "a 2 percent CPI might actually equate to annual price increases of 6 percent or more" (loc. 2578). So the inflation rate is already higher than those in government are willing to admit (loc. 2578). What's more, as money is continually pumped into the system, even the CPI will necessarily rise (loc. 5609). As it does so, investors will get spooked, because they know that rising inflation will kill the value of their investments. The interest rates at which they are willing to lend to the American government will rise: "as the dollar falls, eventually even the CPI–measured inflation rate will rise to unacceptable levels. Then our creditors will no longer be willing to lend us money at such low rates" (loc. 5609).

As interest rates rise, the burden of the government's debt and interest payments will grow larger and larger (loc. 5609). Because creditors will be less willing to invest, the government will have to print the money it needs to make interest payments, thus triggering even more inflation: "the Fed will have to buy any bonds our creditors refuse to roll over. The problem is that the more money the

Fed prints to pay off maturing bonds, the more inflation it must create to buy them" (loc. 5645). Ultimately this will lead to a hyperinflationary tailspin, "as the inflationary fire threatens to burn the dollar and the economy to a cinder" (loc. 5651).

At this point, the government will have but two options, either declare bankruptcy, or allow hyperinflation to utterly destroy the value of the dollar. As Schiff explains, "this is the rock and the hard place the Fed will eventually be between. Whatever it decides to do will set the real crash in motion" (loc. 5651).

5. How America Could Have Avoided the Coming Crash

Now, for Schiff, what the government should have done to avoid this entire situation is that it should have allowed interest rates to rise following the first exploded bubble. This would have allowed a contraction to occur in the short run, yes, but would have spurred a recovery in the long run. Again, the way this works is that rising interest rates encourage savings, and out of these savings comes the capital investment in businesses that spur a recovery (loc. 306–17, 5530–42).

The reason why the government neglected to take this approach, Schiff argues, is because it was unwilling to accept the short term pain that would have been necessary to set this chain of events in motion: "four years ago, I said that the disease in the economy is debt–financed consumption, and that the cure would require a recession. But the medicine I prescribed—Americans consuming less and saving more while companies invest for the long term and the government tightens its belt—was deemed too bitter a pill to swallow by the Bush and Obama administrations. Instead, they fed us bailouts and stimulus to blow the bubble back up. This political aversion to austerity has set us up for an even bigger crash" (loc. 118).

Also at play here is the prevailing opinion that the best way to extricate an economy from a slump is to encourage spending, which the Fed has attempted to do by way of continually lowering interest rates (loc. 311). For Schiff, though, all this does is encourage speculation and debt spending at the expense of savings, thus compounding the problem: "the biggest problem is that savings is the key to economic growth, as it finances capital investment, which leads to job creation and increased output of goods and services. A society that does not save cannot grow. It can fake it for a while, living off foreign savings and a printing press, but such 'growth' is unsustainable" (loc. 317).

6. Why It's Too Late to Avoid the Crash Now

The problem now is that the government debt has become so large that allowing interest rates to rise would make interest payments unmanageable, thus setting off the inflationary spiral outlined above (loc. 202, 5650). And this brings us back to the choice mentioned earlier: either declare bankruptcy or allow hyperinflation to set in. Wait a second though. Isn't there another option? What about the stimulus approach?

a. Government Stimulus Can't Save the Country

Many observers on the left believe that the best way for the government to spur the economy is to pump stimulus dollars into businesses and projects, and thereby create jobs. For Schiff, though, the stimulus approach does not actually create any jobs at all. Rather, it simply transfers resources from one part of the economy to another (loc. 1130). In other words, when the government directs resources to a particular business or project, it may create jobs in that business or project. However, had the government not done this, then the same resources would simply have been directed to other businesses and projects, thus no net benefit is created. This is the case because businesses compete for available resources, so when the government directs resources towards a particular business or project, it takes resources away from other businesses that would have otherwise received it (loc. 1124).

What's more, since the government chooses which businesses and projects to fund based on its preferences, rather than strict profitability, it tends to use up resources in a less efficient way than the market would if left to its own devices. So, for instance, take the solar panel company Solyndra. Solyndra was the recipient of a loan guarantee out of President Obama's $827 billion stimulus package in 2010 (loc. 1091–1104), and subsequently went bankrupt in 2011 (loc. 1111). As Schiff explains, "businesses compete for loans, and the loan guarantee likely helped Solyndra beat out another customer for this loan. The loser was some company that would have gotten the loan if not for the government loan guarantee for Solyndra. That means there was some enterprise—or enterprises—that a bank saw as more financially promising than Solyndra, but the bank went with Solyndra because the government was passing the risk on to taxpayers. So, even if Solyndra hadn't failed, the government would have succeeded only in bringing a new solar panel factory into existence at the expense of some more economically promising undertakings. Instead, the government effectively threw the money into a pit and lit it on fire" (loc. 1130). Schiff concludes with the following advice: "on the jobs situation, the best our politicians can do is get the heck out of the way" (loc. 1173).

For Schiff, though, even the government's getting out of the way now couldn't get the country out of its present predicament. For him, it is simply too late. And this brings us back, once again, to the choice mentioned earlier: either declare bankruptcy or allow hyperinflation to set in. Between the two, Schiff maintains that declaring bankruptcy is vastly preferable.

b. The Government Should Declare Bankruptcy

While the author agrees that declaring bankruptcy is certainly not a welcome move, he insists that it is vastly better than the alternative, which is hyperinflation: "there is simply no way American taxpayers can repay the money the federal government has borrowed. That means our creditors are going to take huge losses. There are really only two questions left unanswered. The first is what form those losses will take. Either our creditors will not get all of their money back, or the money they get back will buy much less than they expect. So either we default, or we allow inflation, but honest repayment isn't an option. Given a choice between the two, default is by far the better choice, even for our creditors" (loc. 5660).

As Schiff notes, declaring bankruptcy does not entail the government's walking away from its creditors entirely; it just means that it will have to restructure its debts in such a way that its creditors will not get everything they're owed (loc. 5666). This leads us to the second question mentioned above; that is, who the government should pay, and what amount: "there's a good debate to have on how we should decide whom to pay and how much... huge profitable banks could get less than old ladies holding on to savings bonds. That might be fairest. Or maybe we give preference to Americans over foreigners... Probably we should treat everyone as equally as possible" (loc. 5673).

PART II: THE SOLUTION

Whether the nation confronts the debt problem head–on, or allows it to fester until it can no longer be ignored, Schiff maintains that the current system is quite simply unsustainable, and things are going to have change in a big way. And the author is not short on ideas here. As mentioned above, Schiff's prescriptions essentially boil down to shrinking government as much as possible, and making it as local as possible. And what exactly might this entail? Here is Schiff's advice in a nutshell and in his own words: "my prescription, at heart, is this: we need to stop bailouts, government spending, government borrowing, and Federal Reserve manipulation of interest rates and debasement of the dollar. We need to reduce government spending so we can offer real tax relief to the productive sectors of our economy. We need to repeal regulations, mandates, and subsidies that create moral hazards, lead to wasteful and inefficient allocation of resources, and artificially drive up the cost of doing business and hiring workers. We need to let wages fall, allow people to pay down debt and start saving, and allow companies to make capital investments so that America can start making things again" (loc. 131). Let's unpack this advice.

Section 1: Curtailing Social Services & Government Regulations

One of Schiff's main prescriptions to reduce the size of government is to have it extricate itself from providing any service that can be provided by the private sector, while at the same time deregulating this private sector. This is necessary for a few different reasons. To begin with, Schiff argues that the private sector is simply more efficient than government at providing services, since competition spurs efficiency, and also because the costs of the services are always borne directly by the person using the service, which discourages waste. In connection with this last point, in the private sector the person paying for the service always has their own money on the line (unlike the case with government bureaucrats) which further discourages waste. In addition to this, the private sector is more efficient the freer it is, so government should not only get out of the business of providing services, it should also lay off from regulating the private sector as much as possible. Second, when government pays for services it must collect taxes in order to do so, and taxes interfere with the free market, which costs jobs and hurts economic growth. Also, because people hate taxes but love getting something for nothing, the government is constantly pressured to spend more on services than it takes in through taxes, and this creates run–away debt (which, as we have seen, is a major problem). Let's take a look at a few examples here.

7. Health Care

Take Health care, for instance. According to Schiff, there is simply no reason why the government should have anything to do with citizens' health insurance, other than to provide it to the most indigent (loc. 3717). By covering individuals' health costs, all the government does, according to Schiff, is raise demand for health services over and above what it would be in a free market, where people and private insurers pay for it directly. By raising demand, the cost of health services goes up, thus making the system more expensive and more burdensome for the taxpayer. By contrast, where people are required to pay their own premiums individually, both private insurers and their clients are more sensitive to cost, which functions to align demand with true market value, thereby reducing cost, and making services less expensive. As Schiff puts it, "the average person has little price sensitivity when it comes to health care. On an aggregate level this means people consume more health care than they normally would. More health–care consumption means increased demand for health care. Increased demand for health care means increased prices for health care. Multiply higher prices by higher use, and you've got the explanation for the growing share of our economy that goes to health care" (loc. 4395).

Now, in a free market system, wealthier individuals would of course be able to afford better health services than the less wealthy, but for Schiff there is no reason why this should be otherwise: "the rich get better versions of lots of things. They drive fancier cars, eat better food, live in more luxurious homes, and wear nicer clothes. That's why we all want to be rich... since we don't feel the need to make sure that nobody has a nicer car than anyone else, why do we feel differently about health care? Inequality in health care is no more a crime than inequality in transportation, shelter, food, or clothing" (loc. 4294). The only real issue, Schiff holds, is whether health care would remain accessible to the poor and middle case; which, according to him, it would. This is the case because, in a private system, health care would be less expensive. And this is not only because in such a system demand comes down to reflect true market value (as we have now seen). There are other factors that would also contribute here, and they mainly have to do with deregulating the private sector.

To begin with, Schiff argues that there are many health services which are now required by law to be performed by a doctor that could very easily be performed just as well and much more inexpensively by less accredited health care professionals: "many routine treatments or procedures can be safely done by non–doctors, and any laws getting in the way of this should be repealed. Do you really need an advanced medical degree to bandage a wound, put in a few stitches, or take blood pressure?... Paramedics, physician's assistants, midwives, nurses, and nurse practitioners must all be given greatly expanded roles if we are ever to begin controlling runaway health–care costs" (loc. 4678). If these reforms were made, then the cost of health services would go down, thus making them more accessible.

Another factor driving up health costs, according to Schiff, is that malpractice rules around doctors are far more onerous than they should be. In other sectors, Schiff explains, issues of malpractice only come up when an individual does not user their best professional judgement, or make their best effort (loc. 4671). When it comes to medicine, though, doctors are liable to be sued even when they make an honest mistake: "it's one thing if a professional in any industry harms someone through malice or negligence. That person should be legally liable. But if someone uses her best professional judgment and is careful, she can still mess up. If she's a doctor, she might be liable for malpractice. We hold doctors to standards of perfection" (loc. 4650).

Because the standards that doctors are held up to is so high, malpractice suits run rampant. As Schiff points out, "in any given year, one in fourteen doctors is hit with a malpractice suit, according to a study in the New England Journal of Medicine" (loc. 4650). This phenomenon drives up costs in two ways. To begin with, doctors are more likely to practice what is called 'defensive medicine'. This is when a doctor performs a procedure not because she thinks it is warranted, but to guard against the possibility of being sued: "what if there's a 100,000,000–to–1 shot that a patient has a specific illness? What if checking on this costs $10,000 and is incredibly time consuming and painful for the patient? Rationally, you would ignore this risk and address more likely risks. But in our world of malpractice litigation run wild, the doctor's incentive is to run the test" (loc. 4657). This, of course, leads to higher costs. Over and above this, because the risk of being sued for malpractice (and the cost thereof) is so high, doctors must raise prices generally in order to cover the risk (loc. 4650). In short, if malpractice rules for doctors were written to be more fair, prices would go done, thus making health services accessible to a yet larger portion of the population.

Finally, if health care were turned over to the private sector and deregulated, government would be able to slash taxes on individuals and businesses, thus leading to more business and employment opportunities, and freeing up more money for individuals to cover their health–insurance costs themselves. Indeed, as Schiff notes, health care is one of the two most expensive government social program (Social Security being the other, which will be discussed next), with Medicare alone costing over $500 billion a year, and that total set to rise to nearly 1 trillion by 2020 (loc. 3710). The payroll taxes imposed to help cover this cost are, the author argues, the single biggest drag on businesses hiring new employees. (1200–25).

And, of course, not having to pay for health care (and the cost of regulating it) would help extricate the government from the massive debt it now faces, which Schiff identifies as the country's most pressing problem.

8. Social Security

Together with health care, Social Security is the most expensive government social program (it cost over $700 billion in 2010); and, for Schiff, is another service the government should have nothing to do with (outside of providing for the indigent in old age). The rationale behind instituting Social Security, Schiff explains, was that people are too irresponsible to save for their own retirement (loc. 3518). But, the author argues, Social Security is already becoming so expensive that the government simply won't be able to meet its payments in the future (loc. 3437–57). What's more, contrary to what many believe, the government hasn't saved any of the money that it has collected over the years to pay for the program (loc. 3524). So, essentially, "the government took money from taxpayers on the premise that they were not smart enough to save for their own retirement, then recklessly spent every dime it took. No matter how irresponsible taxpayers might have been, had the government left them alone, it's clear that they would have done a better job of saving than the government did. After all, the government saved nothing" (loc. 3524).

What's more, the program has taken money out of people's pockets (in the form of taxes) (loc. 3509), and given them a false sense of security (loc. 3509), thus rendering them less able and less likely to have saved additionally for themselves, and leaving in them in still worse a position. Finally, the money that people otherwise would have saved would have been made available to grow businesses and create jobs (loc. 3516). As it is, the government has squandered all of this money away. So, to top it all off, the government "deprived the American economy of all the economic growth retirement savings would have enabled" (loc. 3530).

9. Education

a. K–12

Education is another government service that Schiff attacks. For the author, education is very much like health care, in that it is a service that would be much better provided by the private sector (loc. 4255). For one, the public system is fully protected from competitive pressures, which means that there is really no incentive for it to come up with new and better means of education our youth. And this shows. As Schiff contends, "risk takers and creative thinkers have revolutionized transportation, computing, communications, and most other industries. But in education we're still using the methods developed by John Dewey over a century ago" (loc. 4213). And there is no reason to believe that these methods have achieved their longevity due to their overwhelming success (more on this in a moment). The lack of competitive pressures in the public school system also affects the quality of teachers, as "bad teachers don't lose their jobs, and good teachers don't get raises and promotions" (loc. 4169). What's more, the very lack of a meritocratic system tends to drive out the best and most motivated teachers (loc.4182).

All of this makes it very understandable why America's schools have such a poor track record. Indeed, as the author points out, "less than 40 percent of students scored at or above 'proficient' in mathematics in a 2009 NAEP report. In reading, it's a similar situation, and average scores are not increasing for older students. Only about one quarter of U.S. students are proficient in geography" (loc. 4159). What's more, test scores haven't risen in over thirty years (and in some cases have gone down), despite the fact that spending has done nothing but increase: "one Cato Institute study found that, adjusted for inflation, school spending increased 140 percent between 1970 and 2007, and staff per student increased by more than 75 percent. Meanwhile, looking at the National Assessment of Educational progress tests, reading and math scores were flat, while science scores were down" (loc. 3750).

Of course, Schiff is well aware that abandoning public schools is too extreme a solution for most people (Schiff doesn't actually bring up this point, but the reason why many people object to a fully private school system is that this would tie educational opportunities directly to the means of one's parents, which many see as an unreasonable violation of the principle of equality of opportunity). Given that this is the case, Schiff recommends a compromise in the form of a voucher system as the next best remedy. Under the system the author proposes, parents of school–age children who choose to remove their kids from the public system would be given a voucher representing some portion of the cost the school district would have spent on that student in the course of a school year. So, for instance, "if a school district spends $10,000 per pupil, choose some portion of that—say 50 percent or 75 percent—and allow parents who withdraw their kids from public schools to claim a (taxpayer–funded) voucher for that much money" (loc. 4237). The parent could then use this voucher towards the education of their child through a private institution.

Under this system, public education would be preserved for those who wanted to partake in it. However, a market would also open up for private institutions, which "would spur much of the competition and innovation... described above" (loc. 4243). In order to ensure that private schools charge fully competitive fees, parents could be allowed to use any unused portion of their voucher to set up a savings fund for their child, as "this... would really put pressure on schools to deliver the best education at the lower cost" (loc. 4249). As an added benefit, the public schools would also be forced to compete with the alternatives in the private sector, thus improving the quality of the public system as well (loc. 4249).

b. Higher Education

As for Higher education, Schiff has a different set of reforms in mind here. As the author points out, public opinion has it that a college education is virtually imperative in today's economy. However, Schiff very much challenges this notion. Let's examine. The notion itself comes from a number of different places. Leading the way is the idea that that America is shifting ever more towards a 'knowledge economy', and that it will one day be dominated by 'knowledge jobs', which themselves require a college education. For Schiff, though, the idea that America can or should become a straight–up 'knowledge economy' is silly. Indeed, the author claims that "the push to get everyone going to college and working in 'knowledge jobs' was never grounded in reality" (loc. 4129). The fact is, Schiff continues, the economy will always need a large share of other types of workers: "we need someone to repair broken plumbing. We need someone to tailor suits. Someone needs to mow the high school soccer field, and someone needs to do the landscaping homeowners want. All of these jobs involve skills, and all of them can be very rewarding personally and financially" (loc. 4094). In fact, the author adds, these kinds of skills are often more valuable in starting one's own business than the kinds of skills that are learned in college; and becoming a business owner is often, Schiff claims, "when opportunities really open up" (loc. 4094).

What's more, Schiff maintains that even many knowledge–based–jobs, such as those involving computer programming, can often be more than adequately prepared for through classes in community colleges (loc. 3870); and that still other such jobs are probably best prepared for through on–the–job experience (loc. 3869).

In terms of the value of a higher education, many will point out how those who graduate from college go on to earn much more over the course of their working lives than those who don't (loc. 3770). Even here, though, Schiff questions how much this is a result of the education itself, or the fact that the very qualities that allow one to get into and complete college (such as intelligence, hard work, and having parents who are well–connected [loc. 3776–83]), also allow people to go on to earn more in their careers (loc. 3783–89): "all the factors that make someone more likely to go to college and finish college are also the same factors that, in and of themselves, raise a person's likely income. This fact takes much of the steam out of studies showing a correlation between a college degree and income" (loc. 3796).

Now, for Schiff, it is certainly true that some people stand to benefit a great deal from the college experience: "for a kid with a high IQ, good grades, and high test–scores, college makes sense" (loc. 4084). For many others, though, college is really a waste of time: "if your attention span is short, your study habits incurably bad, or—to be blunt—your IQ is just a bit too low, college probably doesn't promise some great intellectual awakening. Frankly, it means years of struggling and frustration, or alternatively, a college education so simplified that it's nearly worthless" (loc. 3842). This latter point is important. Because the demand for a college education is so high, and so many people attend, the quality of the education must necessarily get watered–down. Also, because so many people end up with college degrees, this dilutes the value of such a degree in and of itself (loc. 3889–97).

As it is now, many end up going to college to receive a watered–down education that does not get them a job when they get out: "given how intellectually barren a college education and how economically worthless a degree is, 'higher education' often amounts to a four–year party. You get drunk on cheap beer, hang out with your friends, and skate on cheap financing and Daddy's money" (loc. 3879). What's more, the time and money it takes to get this education only leaves students deep in debt, and keeps them from having learned useful skills in the meantime (loc. 3851). In addition, the cheap financing mentioned above actually adds to the problem. Indeed, because the government subsidizes student loans, this prompts even more people to attend college than otherwise would (loc. 3950). This compounds the issues mentioned above, and also drives up the cost of a college education (since increasing demand increases the cost), thus driving students deeper into debt (loc. 3950).

The fact is that while college does open up many opportunities, there are many opportunities to be had without a college education (loc. 4090) For Schiff, many individuals should simply forego the college experience in favour of other alternatives. They could enter the workforce sooner, earning valuable experience in the process, and avoid going into debt (loc. 4135). The government could help the process by way of ending subsidized loans (loc. 4109), facilitating apprenticeships and ending minimum wage (loc. 4122). The latter two policies would allow young people to enter the workforce easier (minimum wage will be touched on in greater detail below). Also, it would be a great help if the Fed stopped messing with the interest rate, because this would allow the value of the dollar to inflate, thus encouraging manufacturing to return to the country (loc. 4128). As the numbers attending college drop, so too would the cost, making it more affordable to those who do stand to benefit from the experience (loc. 3950, 4066).

10. The Military

Now, the military is a service that Schiff thinks is best left to the government. Indeed, the author holds that "the single most important function of the federal government is national defense" (loc. 4831). For the author, though, the government still spends far too much here (loc. 4831). For one thing, Schiff argues that America maintains numerous military bases throughout the world that are at best unnecessary, and at worst positively destructive. To take just one example, Schiff asks us to consider the American military base in Germany, where 70,000 troops are kept: "how are we safer for having them there?" he asks, "If we brought them all home, how would the United States be endangered? Maybe we're there to help Germany or other European countries. In that case we should either leave their defense up to them, or send them a bill if they want us to stay" (loc. 4842).

And while this base and others just like it are merely useless, other bases around the world are actually counter–productive. This proves to be the case, Schiff argues, because these bases do nothing other than breed resentment amongst the local population, and invite conflict or the impetus towards it: "many bases around the world are trip wires for future wars. We put our troops in places with a history of violence, possible provoking the locals and setting the stage for a full–fledged conflict. How would you feel if Iran was stationing troops in Canada? Or here? It's not hard for people to see us as colonial occupiers when our soldiers are patrolling their country" (loc. 4848).

And when it comes to the wars that America is waging, or has waged in the recent past, Schiff questions just how valid some of these have been. Since the end of the cold war, the author notes, America has "invaded or bombed Bosnia, Somalia, Kosovo, Iraq, Iraq again, Libya, and in late 2011, Obama even sent U.S. troops to Uganda" (loc. 4879). Now, outside of the second Iraq war, Schiff posits that "the rest of these U.S. invasions had no plausible connection to U.S. security" (loc. 4879), but were fought instead "because their governments are bad governments" (loc. 4879). Now, while Schiff has no intention of defending bad governments, he does question whether America should take on the role of deposing them; for, he says, this ultimately amounts to a doctrine of might makes right, which is arrogant at best, and downright foolhardy at worst (loc. 4879).

Now, Schiff does maintain that sometimes it is choice–worthy to instigate a military action against another country. For him, though, this should require, at a minimum, the support of congress (which most recent wars have not had [loc. 4892]), if not the broad support of the international community: "the first threshold for a U.S. military intervention ought to be a full–fledged congressional declaration of war. And often—especially if it's outside of the Western Hemisphere—we ought to get the rest of the world to agree. To ensure we're not simply enforcing our will, we should get all the major military power on board" (loc. 4898).

11. Private Sector Regulations

In those sectors where government does not involve itself directly, Schiff contends that it still interferes far too much in the form of regulations. Now, Schiff is in the business of financial investing, so he knows first–hand how government regulations affect this industry. And while many believe that the financial sector needs more regulations, the author insists that it is in fact already over–regulated, and needs to be de–regulated in order to be fixed.

a. The Financial Industry

The biggest problem with the financial industry, Schiff argues, is that the major players know that they'll be bailed out if they fail. That is, they know that they are, as the saying goes, 'too big to fail' (loc. 2090). When you combine this with the cheap cash that the Fed provides by way of keeping interest rates low, banks and financial companies are encouraged to speculate more, and take more risks. This creates a toxic and highly dangerous environment (loc. 2090), which, as we have seen, was at the heart of the financial crash of 2008. Without these government policies, Schiff argues, the financial industry would be much less risky, much more stable, and much more efficient. (On the subject of ending bailouts, Schiff maintains that perhaps the best way to do this would be by reintroducing the gold standard. For if the country did this then the Fed would be cut off from printing dollars out of thin air, and the government would no longer have access to the vast sums of money that it uses for the purposes of bailouts, thereby making them impossible [loc. 2184, 2357, 2519, 2555] [more on reinstituting the gold standard below]).

Beyond these policies, though, Schiff argues that the financial industry is rife with regulations that interfere with business, discourage hiring, and prevent it from operating efficiently. From restrictions on hiring practices (loc.1782–88), to operating practices (loc. 1782, 1801–06, 1843–61), to complaint recording procedures (loc. 1813–18) etc. government regulations do far more harm than good, claims Schiff, and it's time they were curtailed. Of course, the author is well aware that the financial industry is not bereft of crooks (loc. 1829). However, Schiff argues that the best approach to this industry (as with most other industries) is to allow market forces to do the regulating (loc. 1734, 1990–2009), and to confront fraudulent operations and cheaters in court, after the fact (loc. 1968, 1990). For the regulatory approach does not stop wrongdoing, and only penalizes honest operations (loc. 1830, 1961).

b. Broad Regulations: Minimum Wage and Anti–Discrimination Laws

Outside of the financial industry, broad regulations affecting all businesses also lead to inefficiencies and destroy jobs and growth, and also often have the reverse effect to what is intended. Two such regulations that will be mentioned here include the minimum wage law and antidiscrimination laws. As for the minimum wage law,

Schiff contends that all it really does is eliminate any job from the economy that employers deem to be worth less than the minimum wage (loc. 1377). Now, many argue that the minimum wage is necessary since people cannot support themselves, much less a family, on anything less. For Schiff, though, minimum wage jobs are primarily entry level jobs that people take when they are young, before they start raising a family, and often even before they leave home (loc. 1406). These jobs are taken not in order to support a family, but to learn important skills that these individuals will need to move up the employment scale, to where they can support a family: "put another way, a young worker provides labor, and most of his compensation comes in the skills he acquires rather than in cash or benefits" (loc.). By introducing minimum wage laws, the government reduces the number of entry level positions; "the result: fewer young American workers possess basic work skills" (loc. 1389). Thus young workers are prevented from acquiring the skills that they will need to move up the employment ladder (loc. 1406).

Another example of a regulation that has the opposite effect to what is intended, and only serves to hurt the economy, are antidiscrimination laws. Antidiscrimination laws often end up discouraging the hiring of minorities, Schiff claims, because employers are afraid of the added potential for lawsuits that comes with laying–off or firing a member of a minority group; an added risk that remains even if the employer is innocent of discrimination, since "even if the government finds no evidence of discrimination, the process is a painful and costly experience for any small business to endure" (loc. 1287).

For Schiff, a far better way to protect minorities from discrimination is by allowing market forces to play out. For, according to him, the absence of regulations here encourages businesses to hire the person who is best for the job, regardless of race, color, creed, sex etc. Indeed, Schiff contends that "any employer who really does discriminate simply based on race or sex is putting bigotry ahead of profit" (loc. 1304), which will hurt his business in the long–run. In the public sector, on the other hand, things are different. Indeed, as Schiff explains, "we need to maintain antidiscrimination laws in public sectors... as there are no market–based safeguards to punish bad behavior by government employers" (loc. 1304).

Again, as government eases up on its regulations, the taxes needed to enforce them will go down, thus leading to even more job opportunities and economic growth. In addition, because government spending will go down, the opportunity for government to accrue large debt will also go down, thus helping solve this problem as well.

Section 2: The Gold Standard, Tax Reform, and Localizing Government

12. Reinstituting the Gold Standard

Even if the reforms mentioned above were instituted, as long as governments are around, and people like getting something for nothing (meaning forever and a day), Schiff contends that political parties will always be tempted to reintroduce costly and ultimately unsustainable social programs, and people will always be willing to vote for them. Of course, if the government (or at least the Fed) were not allowed to print money whenever it was convenient to do so (meaning whenever the government wants cash), this could not happen. So, for this reason, Schiff advocates cutting this avenue off by way of reintroducing the gold standard. That is, having every American dollar backed, and capable of being exchanged (by the Fed) for a fixed amount of gold. (As mentioned above, reintroducing the gold standard would also have the effect of eliminating government bailouts from the realm of possibility, which, for Schiff, is another point in favour of going back to gold). Now, the American dollar was actually on the gold standard until 1971; but in that year, President Nixon abolished it (loc. 2301). Let's start from the beginning though.

a. A Short History of the Federal Reserve

The Federal Reserve was established in 1913 in order to act as the banker's bank, and to create a common currency that would be accepted by all and sundry across the land (loc. 622). How this worked was that "banks could deposit some of their assets—commercial paper or gold—with the Fed, and the Fed in return would issue its own bank notes to the individual bank" (loc. 622). Originally, the Fed was required to back whatever bank notes (U.S. dollars) it issued, with the paper money and gold that it received from other banks. To be precise, "each Federal Reserve Note was backed 40 percent by gold and 100 percent by commercial paper (loans from other banks)" (loc. 629). This meant that the Fed was limited in how many bank notes (dollars) it could issue (each note had to backed by something tangible, after all).

At first, the Fed was actually restricted from buying government bonds (loc. 646). However, WWI soon came around (the very next year in fact!), and the government needed some money. And since it was war time and all, it was deemed necessary for the Fed to relax its rules and lend to the government by way of buying up government–issued Treasury bonds (loc. 646). And how did the Fed pay for the bonds? It printed the money (loc. 652). And, of course, since the Fed was printing the money to fund a loan, the money wasn't actually backed up by anything (except a government IOU). The rule was allowed to slip, but only for a little while, because the money would be paid back right after the war after all. And the money was paid back after the war (loc. 687).

However, by the 1920's the Fed returned to printing unbacked money (again at the behest of the government); this time to help Great Britain, who was reeling badly following the war (loc. 712, 2295). As Schiff explains, "from mid–1921 to mid–1929, the Fed increased the money supply by 55 percent" (loc. 718). For Schiff, all this extra credit flowing about in the economy led directly to the stock market bubble that built up throughout the roaring 20's, and that finally popped in 1929 (loc. 722).

But the Fed didn't stop printing unbacked dollars then. Indeed, as Schiff explains, this practice continued all of the way up to 1971 (loc. 749, 2301), when the government officially took the dollar off the gold standard, allowing it to float freely (loc. 2301, 2307). Now, at the time, many people (including Alan Greenspan) noted the danger of removing the dollar entirely from the gold standard, because this essentially gave the Fed a free ticket to print money whenever it saw fit (loc. 2314). This is a problem because if money is printed faster than an economy grows, this creates inflation, and too much inflation, as we have seen, can destroy an economy. In order to assuage these fears, the Fed made a commitment to keep inflation low, at roughly 2 percent per year.

Now, the Fed has been relatively successful in sticking to this commitment up to this point. For Schiff though, the government has now run up so much debt that this is ultimately a commitment that is going to be impossible for the Fed to keep into the future (as we have seen). And it is this, Schiff thinks, that will ultimately cause the real crash. The best way to avoid this situation again, Schiff holds, is to make sure the dollar is backed by something, which is why he favors bringing back the gold standard.

13. Tax Reform

Another reform that Schiff recommends is changing how the government collects its taxes. At the moment most of the government's tax proceeds come from income and payroll taxes. Indeed, as the author points out, "60 percent of all taxes are direct taxes on wages. Twenty percent of all tax receipts are the employer portion of payroll taxes, and nine percent are corporate income taxes" (loc. 2716). For Schiff, there is absolutely no good reason why government should collect taxes off income. Instead, he maintains that government services should, as much as possible, be covered by user fees, and, where this is not possible, by sales taxes and import taxes.

According to Schiff, the reason why income taxes are so bad is because they essentially penalize work, and this is the last thing that should be penalized (loc. 2716). Instead, services should be paid for directly by those who use them, through user fees (loc. 2667). For instance, highways should be paid for through tolls (loc. 2746), and city streets should be paid for through congestion fees (loc. 2765) (both of which forms of payment are becoming easier now due to new communications and digital technologies [loc. 2758]); public transit should be paid for through fares (loc. 2772); the postal service should be paid for through shipping fees (loc. 2778); and parks should be paid for through user fees (loc. 2778) etc.

For those services that cannot be paid for at the point of service, the next best thing, according to Schiff, is to collect the money for their maintenance through sales taxes. Consumption is the most appropriate part of the economy to tax, claims Schiff, because it is the least productive: "why do we tax savings, investment, and productive labor? Taxing any economic activity or asset ownership is bad. But when we need taxes, we should try to tax the least valuable economic activity. And that's consumption. When you work, you create value. When you save, you provide the opportunity for future capital investment. When you invest, you provide capital for others to create new efficiencies. Consumption is the least economically productive activity" (loc. 2789).

Of course, Schiff is well aware that this is exactly the opposite of what most experts believe. Indeed, the author points out on numerous occasions how politicians like to advise the populace to get out and spend whenever the economy is in trouble (loc. 311–31). For Schiff, though, saving is far more important when you are trying to get out of a slump (as we have seen); and, in general, spending and saving need to be balanced out, and a consumption tax is the best way to achieve this (loc. 2795–2827).

14. Localizing Government

As mentioned in the opening paragraph, Schiff's two guiding principles with regards to government is that it should be kept as small as possible and as local as possible. Up until now, we have focused mainly on Schiff's prescriptions with regards to how to keep government as small as possible. We will now say a few words with regards to keeping it as local as possible.

Government should be localized as much as possible, according to Schiff, first and foremost because the values and concerns of a population differ from place to place. Given that this is the case, by dealing with policy matters at as local a level as possible you ensure that people's particular values and concerns are respected as much as possible. In other words, it's a matter of freedom: "it's easier for laws to match public opinion when the laws cover fewer people" (loc. 4769).

Also, the more power you give municipalities and states to write their own laws, the more they will differ one from the other. This is beneficial on two counts. First, it opens up the possibility for people who are unhappy with the laws of their particular municipality or state to simply pick up and move to another where the laws suit their fancy more. For Schiff, "this matters when it comes to public policy because the right to choose your government is a crucial part of being free" (loc. 4749). Second, having different municipalities and states with different laws is beneficial because it allows for policy competition; that is, it allows us to test out which laws work best, and to learn from our mistakes: "you sometimes hear the phrase 'laboratory of democracy' used to describe these ideas. Different states can try different ideas, and we can watch which ones get the best results" (loc. 4775). And this policy competition can also extend to municipalities (loc. 4775).

Now, being the freedom lover pragmatist that he is, Schiff thinks that the government should keep its nose out of most things, including things like prostitution (loc. 5069–76), gambling (loc. 5125), and (to a certain extent) abortion (loc. 5166–80) and drugs (loc. 5040–63). For him, though, what is really best is that these matters be left up to state governments, in order that people's opinions in different regions be respected as much as possible.

15. Conclusion

While Schiff believes that shrinking government is the right thing to do on both practical and ideological grounds, he is convinced that the fact that government has grown so large now (and especially in terms of its debt), that a major crash is inevitable. As such, he recommends that the American government declare bankruptcy, renegotiate its debts, and start anew on the bedrock of market forces and federalism.

*For more from Peter Schiff, Here is a link to his channel on YouTube: http://www.youtube.com/user/schiffreport?ob=4&feature=results_main

*For more great summaries of non-fiction books (including a new one every two weeks) visit http://newbooksinbrief.com/

33633859R00022

Made in the USA
San Bernardino, CA
06 May 2016